ICKY BUG

Numbers

1 2 3 4 5

by Jerry Pallotta
Illustrated by David Biedrzycki and Rob Bolster

SCHOLASTIC INC.

New York   Toronto   London   Auckland   Sydney   Mexico City   New Delhi   Hong Kong   Buenos Aires

Thank you to Wilbert Morgan, Gloria Canada, Richard Jenisch, and Marilyn Denison.
—— *Jerry Pallotta*

To the Ceccaci's, Butch, Diane, Laura, and Patrick. Always number one in my book.
—— David Biedrzycki

Thank you, Dave, for your work on this "ICKY" book.
—— *Rob Bolster*

Thank you to Ralph Masiello who illustrated most of the bug faces
on the last page of this book.

Text copyright © 2003 by Jerry Pallotta.
Illustrations copyright © 2003 by David Biedrzycki and Rob Bolster.
All rights reserved. Published by Scholastic Inc.
SCHOLASTIC and associated logos are trademarks
and/or registered trademarks of Scholastic Inc.
Icky Bug ® is a Registered Trademark of Jerry Pallotta.

ISBN 0-439-56010-1

12 11 10 9 8 7   8/0

Printed in the U.S.A   08
First printing, November 2003

zero

one

Let's learn about numbers and icky bugs, too.
The first number is zero. There are no icky bugs on the red zero.
The next number is one. One black ant is walking on the orange number one.
One! Count it!

two

three

Two pretty blue butterflies flew onto the yellow number two.
Count them! One, two!
One, two, three yellow moths sit on the light purple number three.

four

five

There are one, two, three, four caterpillars creeping along the blue four.
Five flies are buzzing around the green number five.

six   seven

One, two, three, four, five, six beetles scurry on the purple number six.
Seven spiders tiptoe on the light green number seven.
Count them: One, two, three, four, five, six, seven!

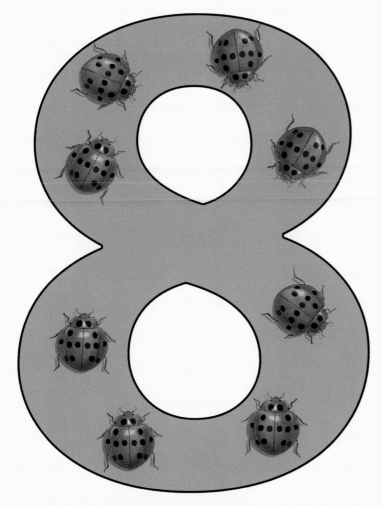

eight

nine

Eight ladybird beetles landed on the aqua number eight.
Count them. Nine shield bugs jump on the gold number nine.
Count these, too!

10

ten

Yea! Now we are at the number ten.
Ten dragonflies just zigzagged in and landed near the pink number ten.
Count: one, two, three, four, five, six, seven, eight, nine, ten!

10 9 8 7 6 5 4 3 2 1

You are so good at counting to ten. Now, try counting backward using different icky bugs. Ten, nine, eight, seven, six, five, four, three, two, one!

Are you having fun counting? Then count some more!
Count the bugs on and around each number.

Now, count the bugs that are alike. It does not matter where they are on these two pages. How many ants did you count? How many caterpillars? How many spiders? Did you count any other bugs?

Let's play another game.
Can you find a beetle with 2 feathery antennae,
and a dragonfly with 4 wings?

Now look for a moth with 6 ovals,
a spider with 8 legs,
and a ladybird beetle with 10 spots!

Can you also find an icky bug with 1 very long, skinny body,
and a bee with 3 yellow stripes?

Can you find a beetle with 5 green stripes,
a ladybug with 7 spots,
and a beetle with 9 yellow triangles on its body?

You counted the numbers from one to ten. Now count to twenty!
One, two, three, four, five, six, seven, eight, nine, ten.
Ten kissing bugs march around the yellow number twenty.

Twenty

Another group of ten march around the word twenty. Eleven, twelve, thirteen, fourteen, fifteen, sixteen, seventeen, eighteen, nineteen, twenty. You did it! You counted and read all the way to TWENTY!

skip count even numbers

1

2

3

4

5

Skip counting
is when you skip over a number.
You will skip every other number
all the way to twenty.
This is the same as
counting even numbers.
Ready? Go!
Two, four, six, eight, ten!

10

9

8

7

6

Twelve, fourteen, sixteen, eighteen, TWENTY!
You counted the butterflies and skipped over the beetles.

skip count odd numbers

1

2

3

4

5

6

7

8

Now skip count the ladybugs,
starting with the number one.
You are skipping the wasps. One, three, five, seven.

9
10
11
12
13
14

Nine, eleven, thirteen, fifteen, seventeen, nineteen!
Skip counting by twos starting with the number
one is the same as counting odd numbers!

15
16
20
19
18
17

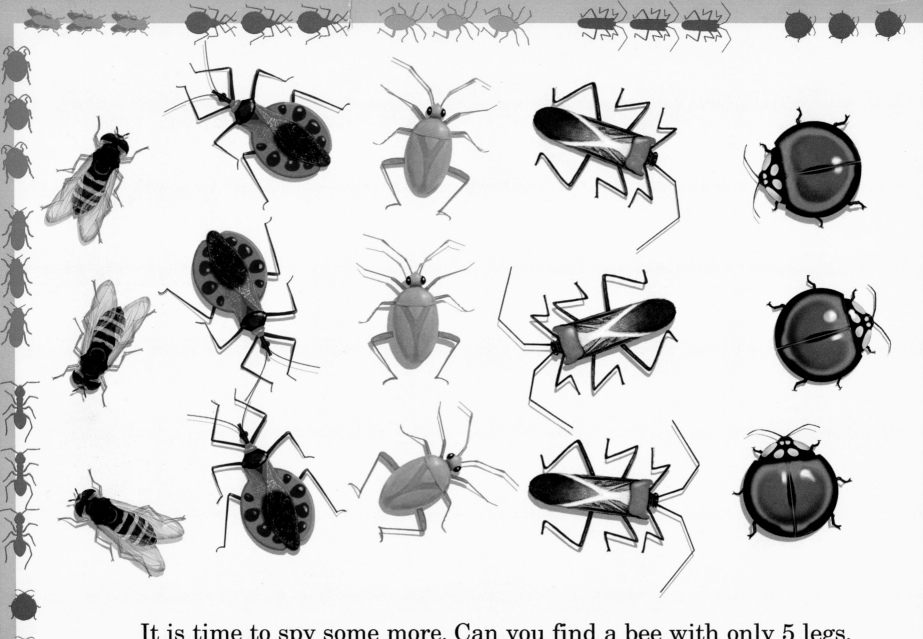

It is time to spy some more. Can you find a bee with only 5 legs, and a true bug with 1 antenna? How many bugs have 6 legs? Do not count the icky bugs in the borders.

Count the 12 butterfly wings. Find the ant with 2 short antennae,
but count all the antennae on these 15 icky bugs.
Count the green stripes on the 3 potato beetles.

$$2 + 1 = 3$$

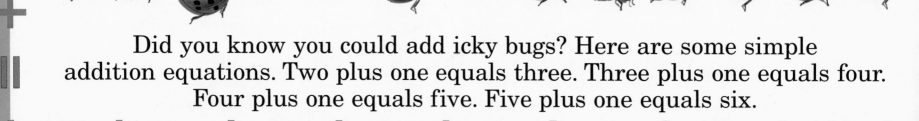

$$3 + 1 = 4$$

$$4 + 1 = 5$$

$$5 + 1 = 6$$

Did you know you could add icky bugs? Here are some simple addition equations. Two plus one equals three. Three plus one equals four. Four plus one equals five. Five plus one equals six.

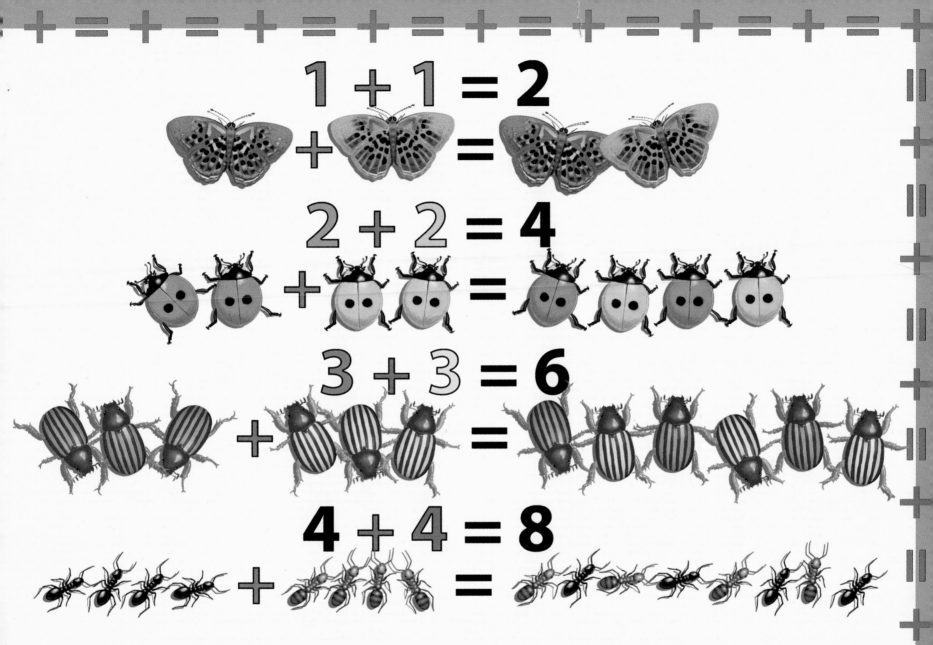

$$1 + 1 = 2$$

$$2 + 2 = 4$$

$$3 + 3 = 6$$

$$4 + 4 = 8$$

Here are some more addition problems:
One plus one equals two. Two plus two equals four.
Three plus three equals six. Four plus four equals eight.

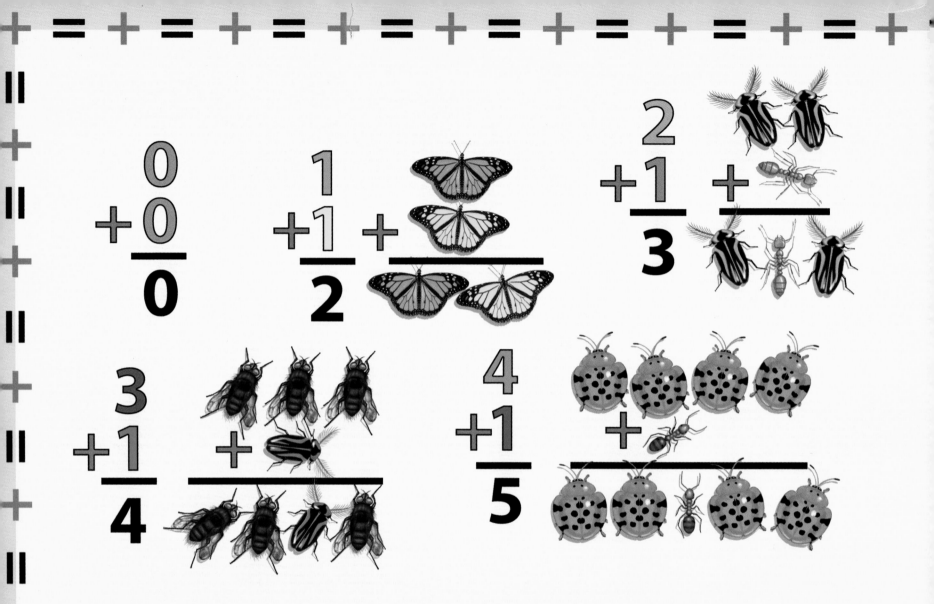

$$+\dfrac{\begin{matrix}0\\0\end{matrix}}{0}$$

$$+\dfrac{\begin{matrix}1\\1\end{matrix}}{2}\quad+$$

$$+\dfrac{\begin{matrix}2\\1\end{matrix}}{3}\quad+$$

$$+\dfrac{\begin{matrix}3\\1\end{matrix}}{4}\quad+$$

$$+\dfrac{\begin{matrix}4\\1\end{matrix}}{5}\quad+$$

Equations can be shown up and down, too!
Zero plus zero equals zero. One plus one equals two.
Two plus one equals three. Three plus one equals four.
Four plus one equals five.

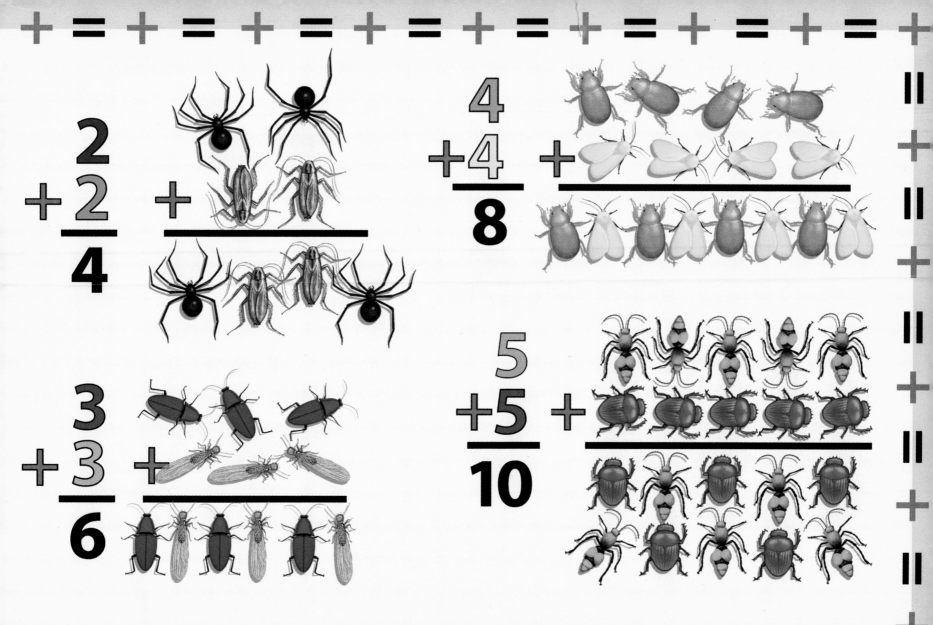

Two plus two equals four. Three plus three equals six.
Four plus four equals eight. Five plus five equals ten.

Here is some subtraction. Subtraction is taking away.
This spider has caught seven flies in its web.
Three cocoons are being saved. Four ants are being careful.

7−2=5

3−1=2

Did two flies escape, or did the spider eat them?
Seven minus two equals five.
One cocoon is missing. Three minus one equals two.
Three ants went home. Four minus three equals one.

4−3=1

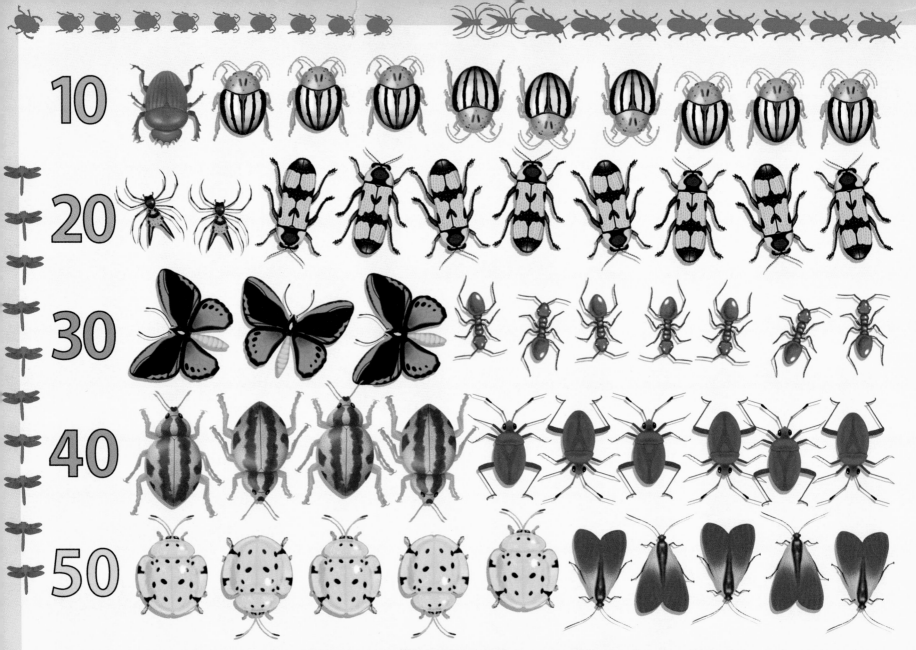

10

20

30

40

50

Now count by tens. Pay attention and look for patterns.
TEN, TWENTY, THIRTY, FORTY, FIFTY,

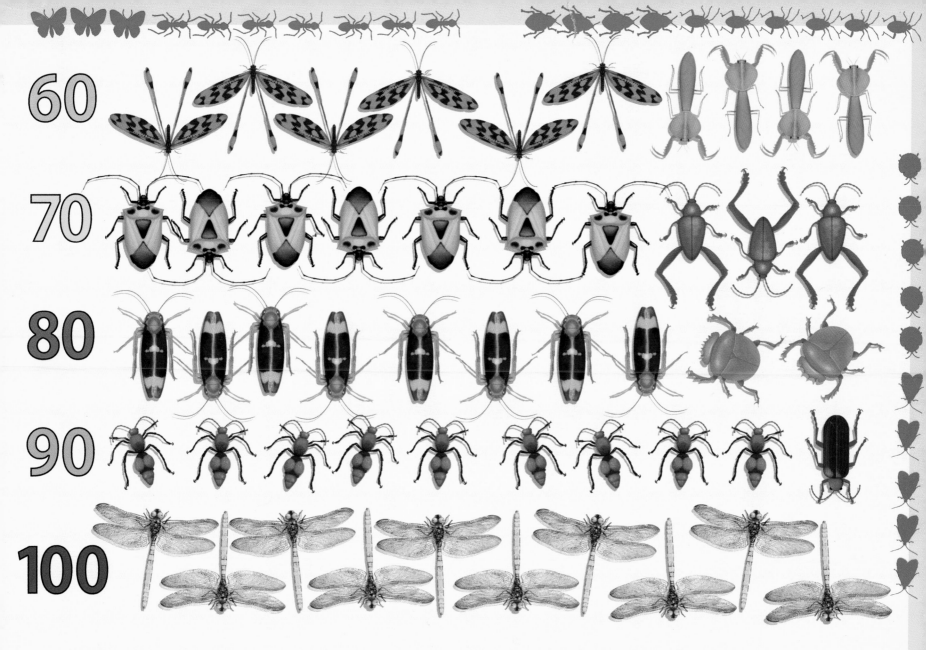

60

70

80

90

100

SIXTY, SEVENTY, EIGHTY, NINETY, ONE HUNDRED ICKY BUGS!
Look back. We counted by ones, by twos, and now by tens. Great job!

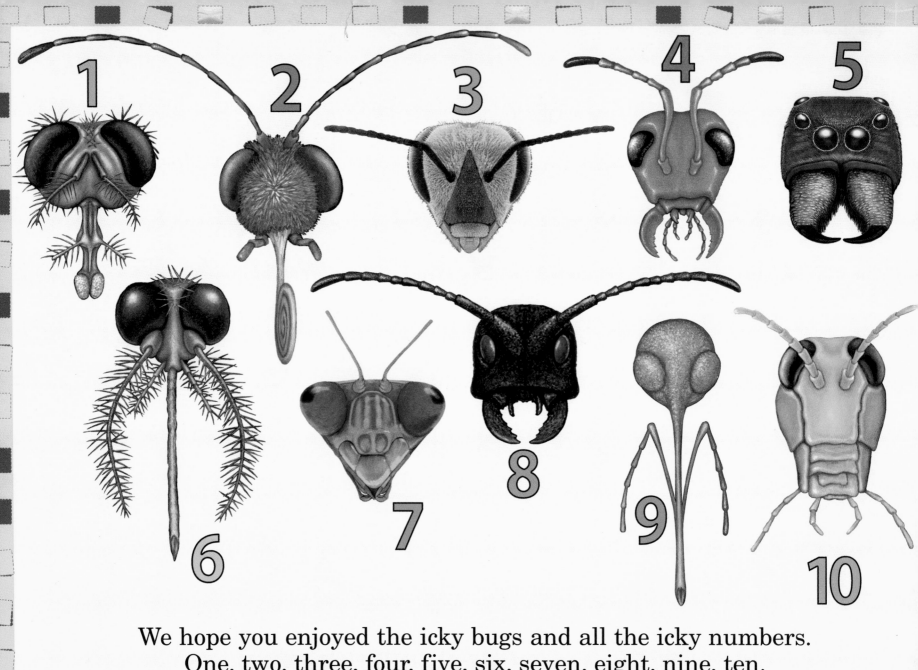

We hope you enjoyed the icky bugs and all the icky numbers.
One, two, three, four, five, six, seven, eight, nine, ten.
Which icky bug face is your icky favorite?